MEZE

Mediterranean-style eating

Your Promise of Success

Welcome to the world of Confident Cooking, created for you in
our test kitchen, where recipes are double-tested by our team
of home economists to achieve a high standard of success.

MURDOCH BOOKS®

Sydney • London • Vancouver • New York

Meze on the Menu

The open air and sunshine inspires us all to entertain outside. While the trusty barbecue is a reliable standby, it's good to tempt our tastebuds with something a little different from time to time.

WHAT IS MEZE?

Combine the rich colours and textures that are typical of Mediterranean countries, relaxing with good friends, cool drinks and dappled sunshine and you're nearly there. Meze is more than a style of food—it's a unique eating experience, a celebration of flavours from Greece, Turkey and the Middle East.

The literal translation from Greek is 'tasty morsels' that are designed to whet your appetite before a main meal. But more and more, we are finding that meze platters make a simply magnificent meal in their own right. There are no rules to tell you how to put together a meze platter—you can be as adventurous as you like.

OILS AIN'T OILS

Much of the preparation for a meze platter can be done in advance as the food can be served cold, warm or hot. This means you can relax with your friends as you offer them such temptations as kebabs, dolmades, bean dishes, dips and breads, marinated vegetables and seafood. And your guests don't need to

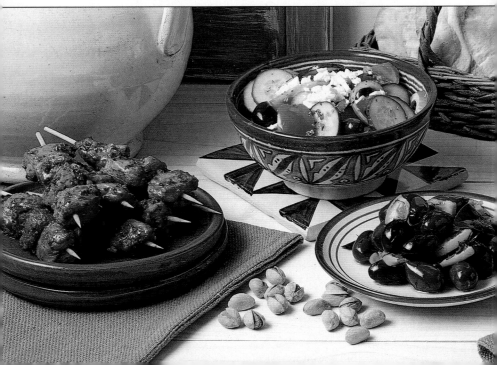

feel guilty if they squeeze in 'just one more' as Mediterranean cuisine is very healthy, predominantly made up of fish, vegetables, pulses and rice, and only small amounts of red meat and dairy products. Olive oil features in almost every dish. It complements the flavours of the other ingredients, and adds a little fruitiness of its own, without being overpowering. Better still, it has no cholesterol, which contributes to Mediterranean countries having a low incidence of heart disease.

MEZE—THE COMPLETE DINING EXPERIENCE

Meze is not restricted to finger food. Soups, salads and breads can help make it a full and satisfying meal. If you are planning to serve meze to four people as a main meal, a rough guide would be to allow about two recipes per person (giving you a total of eight different dishes) served with plenty of crusty bread. Tradition suggests that all the meze plates should be brought out together, allowing you and your guests to have a relaxed meal, picking at a variety of dishes, but this is entirely up to you. Chilled retsina is the perfect accompaniment to the rich flavours of a meze platter. Or, for something completely different, try the unique licorice flavour of ouzo. Served straight or with a little iced water, it is a delicious and authentic accompaniment.

From left to right: Souvlakia; Greek village salad; Dill, garlic and orange marinated olives; Tabbouleh; Vegetarian dolmades; cubes of Greek feta.

Meze

Select a few of our tempting recipes to make a meze platter that will delight (not to mention impress) your friends.

Grilled lamb kofta

Preparation time:
  20 minutes +
  1 hour soaking
Total cooking time:
  10 minutes
Makes 8

400 g lean lamb mince
1 tablespoon chopped
  fresh flat-leaf parsley
1 teaspoon ground
  cumin
2 tablespoons chopped
  fresh coriander
pinch of cayenne pepper
2 cloves garlic, crushed
1/2 teaspoon dried mint
3/4 cup (185 g) thick
  Greek-style yoghurt

1. Soak eight 15 cm skewers in water for 1 hour, or until they sink, to ensure that they don't burn during cooking.
2. Combine the lamb mince, parsley, cumin, coriander, cayenne pepper, half the garlic and 1/2 teaspoon salt in a bowl and knead the mixture by hand for a few minutes until smooth and the mixture leaves the side of the bowl.
3. Divide the mixture into 16 portions. With cool, clean hands, roll each portion into a ball. Thread two balls onto each prepared skewer, moulding each ball into an oval shape 4–5 cm long.
4. Combine the dried mint, yoghurt and remaining clove of garlic in a bowl. Season with salt and pepper.
5. Heat a lightly oiled barbecue hot plate until hot or heat a grill to its highest setting. Cook the kofta for about 6 minutes, turning once. Serve hot with yoghurt mint sauce.

NUTRITION PER KOFTA
Protein 12 g; Fat 2.5 g; Carbohydrate 1 g; Dietary Fibre 0 g; Cholesterol 35 mg; 325 kJ (80 cal)

Grilled lamb kofta

Cauliflower fritters

Preparation time:
  15 minutes +
  30 minutes standing
Total cooking time:
  15 minutes
Serves 4–6

600 g cauliflower
1/2 cup (55 g) besan
  flour
2 teaspoons ground
  cumin
1 teaspoon ground
  coriander
1 teaspoon ground
  turmeric
pinch cayenne pepper
1 egg, lightly beaten
1 egg yolk
oil, for deep-frying

1. Cut the cauliflower into bite-sized florets. Sift the flour and spices into a bowl, then stir in 1/2 teaspoon salt.
2. Lightly whisk 1/4 cup (60 ml) water, the beaten egg and egg yolk in a jug. Make a well in the centre of the dry ingredients and pour in the egg mixture, mixing with a whisk until smooth. Stand for 30 minutes.
3. Fill a deep pan one-third full of oil and heat until a cube of bread dropped into the oil browns in 15 seconds.

Holding the florets by the stem, dip them into the batter, allowing the excess batter to drain back into the bowl. Deep-fry in batches for 3–4 minutes, or until puffed and browned. Drain, sprinkle with salt and serve hot.

NUTRITION PER SERVE (6)
Protein 5 g; Fat 5 g;
Carbohydrate 7 g; Dietary
Fibre 3 g; Cholesterol
60 mg; 390 kJ (95 cal)

Note: Besan flour is chickpea flour and is available at health food stores.

Stuffed zucchini flowers

Preparation time:
  1 hour 20 minutes
  + 1 hour standing
Total cooking time:
  10 minutes
Makes 24

1 1/2 cups (185 g)
  plain flour
7 g dry yeast or
  15 g compressed
  fresh yeast
24 zucchini with flowers
50 g kefalotyri cheese
20 g (8) anchovy fillets
oil, for deep-frying

1. Sift the flour and 1/4 teaspoon salt into a bowl and make a well in the centre. Whisk the yeast and 1 1/4 cups (315 ml) warm water in a bowl until dissolved and pour into the well. Gradually stir with the whisk to form a thick, tacky batter. Cover with plastic wrap and leave in a warm place for 1 hour, or until frothy. Do not stir.
2. Gently open the zucchini flowers and remove the centre stamens. Wash and drain dry. Cut the cheese into 1 cm cubes. Drain the anchovy fillets and cut into 1 1/2 cm pieces.
3. Put a cube of cheese and a piece of anchovy into the centre of each flower. Re-form the petals around them. Fill a deep pan one-third full of oil and heat until a cube of bread dropped into the oil browns in 15 seconds. Dip the flowers into the batter, turning to coat and drain off the excess. Deep-fry in batches for 1–2 minutes, or until puffed and lightly brown. Drain. Serve hot.

NUTRITION PER SERVE
Protein 2 g; Fat 1.5 g;
Carbohydrate 5.5 g; Dietary
Fibre 0.5 g; Cholesterol
2.5 mg; 195 kJ (45 cal)

Note: Kefalotyri is a pale hard sheep's milk cheese. If unavailable, Parmesan or pecorino can be substituted.

Cauliflower fritters (top) and
Stuffed zucchini flowers

Vegetarian dolmades

Preparation time:
1 hour + cooling time
Total cooking time:
1 hour 5 minutes
Makes 20–25

1/2 cup (125 ml) olive oil
6 spring onions, chopped
3/4 cup (150 g) long-grain rice
1/4 cup (15 g) chopped fresh mint
2 tablespoons chopped fresh dill
2/3 cup (170 ml) lemon juice
1/4 cup (35 g) currants
1/4 cup (40 g) pine nuts
240 g (about 50) packaged vine leaves
2 tablespoons olive oil, extra

1. Heat the oil in a pan. Add the spring onion and cook over medium heat for 1 minute. Stir in the rice, mint, dill, half the lemon juice, and season to taste. Add 1 cup (250 ml) water and bring to the boil, then reduce the heat, cover and simmer for 20 minutes. Remove the lid, fork through the currants and pine nuts, cover with a paper towel, then the lid and leave to cool.
2. Rinse the vine leaves under water and gently separate. Drain, then dry on paper towels. Trim any thick stems with scissors. Line the base of a 20 cm pan (with a lid) with any torn or misshapen leaves. Choose the larger leaves for filling and use smaller leaves to patch up any gaps.
3. Place each leaf shiny-side-down. Spoon a tablespoon of filling into the centre, bring in the sides and roll up tightly from the stem end. Place seam-side-down with the stem end closest to you in the base of the pan, tightly in a single layer.
4. Pour in the rest of the lemon juice, the extra oil and about 3/4 cup (185 ml) water to just cover the dolmades. Cover with an inverted plate and place a tin on the plate to firmly compress the dolmades. Cover with the lid.
5. Bring to the boil, then reduce the heat and simmer for 45 minutes. Allow to cool in the pan. Serve at room temperature.

NUTRITION PER SERVE
Protein 1.5 g; Fat 7.5 g; Carbohydrate 5.5 g; Dietary Fibre 0 g; Cholesterol 0 mg; 380 kJ (90 cal)

Note: The dolmades will store, covered in the cooking liquid, in the refrigerator for up to 2 weeks.

Vegetarian dolmades

Line the base of the pan with any torn or misshapen leaves.

Trim any thick stems from the vine leaves with kitchen scissors.

Bring in the sides of the leaves and roll up tightly from the stem end.

Put the dolmades seam-side-down into the pan, fitting them tightly in a single layer.

Baked eggplant

Preparation time:
  40 minutes +
  30 minutes standing
Total cooking time:
  1 hour 20 minutes
Serves 6

6 slender eggplants
*1/3 cup (80 ml) olive
  oil*
2 onions, halved and
  sliced
2 cloves garlic, crushed
1 ripe tomato, finely
  chopped
1 tablespoon finely
  chopped fresh flat-leaf
  parsley
1 teaspoon chopped
  fresh dill
*1/4 teaspoon ground
  cinnamon*
1 teaspoon paprika
1/4 teaspoon sugar
2 tablespoons currants
1 tomato, extra,
  halved, grated and
  skin discarded

1. Make two deep cuts
lengthways in each
eggplant to make
pockets without cutting
all the way through.
Hold open the pockets
and sprinkle generously
with salt. Leave in a
colander for 30 minutes,
then rinse well and
drain on paper towels.
2. Heat half the oil in
a frying pan, add the
onion and cook over
low heat for 20 minutes,
or until very soft. Add
the garlic and cook for
a further 5 minutes.
Increase the heat to
medium and add the
tomato, parsley, dill,
cinnamon, paprika,
sugar and currants.
Cook for 10 minutes,
or until thick and
pulpy. Taste before
seasoning. Preheat
the oven to moderate
180°C (350°F/Gas 4).
3. Heat the remaining
oil over medium heat
in a large frying pan
and brown the eggplant
all over for about
10 minutes, or until
the skin has changed
colour and the
eggplants are soft.
Drain on paper towels.
4. Put the eggplants in
an ovenproof dish large
enough to fit them in a
single layer. Carefully
open the pockets and
spoon in the filling
(or use your fingers).
Spoon the grated tomato
around the eggplant
and bake, covered, for
20 minutes. Uncover
and bake for a further
15 minutes. Delicious
served warm or at
room temperature.

NUTRITION PER SERVE
*Protein 2.5 g; Fat 13 g;
Carbohydrate 6.5 g; Dietary
Fibre 4 g; Cholesterol
0 mg; 630 kJ (150 cal)*

---

*Baked eggplant (top) and
Fried chickpeas*

Fried chickpeas

Preparation time:
  30 minutes +
  overnight soaking
Total cooking time:
  15 minutes
Serves 5

285 g dried chickpeas
oil, for deep-frying
1/2 teaspoon paprika
*1/4 teaspoon cayenne
  pepper*

1. Soak the chickpeas
in plenty of cold water
overnight. Drain well.
2. Fill a deep pan one-
third full of oil and heat
until a cube of bread
dropped into the oil
browns in 15 seconds.
Deep-fry half the
chickpeas for 3 minutes.
Drain and repeat with
the rest of the chickpeas.
Partially cover the deep
fryer as some beans
may pop. Don't leave
the oil unattended.
3. Deep-fry the
chickpeas again in
batches for 3 minutes
each batch, or until
browned. Drain.
Season the paprika
with salt and cayenne
pepper, and sprinkle
over the chickpeas
while still hot. Cool
before serving.

NUTRITION PER SERVE
*Protein 3.5 g; Fat 5 g;
Carbohydrate 7.5 g; Dietary
Fibre 2.5 g; Cholesterol
0 mg; 375 kJ (90 cal)*

Mushrooms in red wine

Preparation time:
  15 minutes +
  overnight marinating
Total cooking time:
  30 minutes
Serves 6

400 g cap mushrooms
20 g butter
1 tablespoon olive oil
4 small brown pickling
  onions, quartered
1 bay leaf
$^1/2$ cup (125 ml) dry
  red wine
1 tablespoon lemon
  juice
1 tablespoon chopped
  fresh dill
2 tablespoons chopped
  fresh coriander

1. Trim the stalks and halve the mushrooms.
2. Melt the butter and oil in a large heavy-based pan. When foaming, add the onions, and toss over medium heat for 2 minutes, or until starting to brown. Add the mushrooms. Cook for 2–3 minutes, or until they are beginning to soften and brown.
3. Add the bay leaf, wine and lemon juice. Bring to the boil, then reduce the heat to low and simmer, covered, for 25 minutes, or until the mushrooms are tender. Remove the bay leaf and stir in the dill and coriander. Taste before seasoning with salt and cracked black pepper. Transfer to an airtight container and marinate the mushrooms in the refrigerator overnight or for up to 2 days. Delicious served hot or cold.

NUTRITION PER SERVE
*Protein 2.5 g; Fat 3 g;
Carbohydrate 2.5 g; Dietary
Fibre 2 g; Cholesterol
8.5 mg; 260 kJ (60 cal)*

Zucchini patties

Preparation time:
  20 minutes
Total cooking time:
  15 minutes
Makes 16

2 medium zucchini,
  grated
1 small onion, grated
$^1/4$ cup (30 g) self-
  raising flour
$^1/3$ cup (35 g) grated
  kefalotyri cheese or
  Parmesan
1 tablespoon chopped
  fresh mint
2 teaspoons chopped
  fresh parsley
pinch ground nutmeg
$^1/4$ cup (25 g) dry
  breadcrumbs
1 egg
olive oil, for shallow-
  frying

1. Put the zucchini and onion into the centre of a clean tea towel, twist as tightly as possible and squeeze dry. Combine the zucchini, onion, flour, cheese, mint, parsley, nutmeg, breadcrumbs and egg in a large bowl. Season well with salt and cracked black pepper, and mix with clean hands to a stiff mixture that clumps together.
2. Heat the shallow-frying oil in a large pan over medium heat. Drop level tablespoons of the mixture into the pan and shallow-fry for 2–3 minutes, or until well browned all over. Drain well on paper towels and serve hot. The patties can be served plain sprinkled with salt or are delicious served with tzatziki (see page 49).

NUTRITION PER SERVE
*Protein 2.5 g; Fat 2 g;
Carbohydrate 3 g; Dietary
Fibre 0.5 g; Cholesterol
13 mg; 165 kJ (40 cal)*

Note: Kefalotyri and kefalograviera are pale hard sheep's milk cheeses originating in Greece. In this recipe, Parmesan or pecorino cheeses may be substituted.

*Mushrooms in red wine (top) and
Zucchini patties*

With clean hands, roll the wheat mixture into a smooth sausage shape.

Make a hole with your forefinger and gently work into a shell.

Kibbeh

Preparation time:
45 minutes + 2 hours
refrigeration
Total cooking time:
25 minutes
Makes 15

1^1/3 *cups (235 g) fine
burghul wheat*
150 g lean lamb, chopped
1 onion, grated
2 tablespoons plain flour
1 teaspoon ground allspice

Filling
2 teaspoons olive oil
1 small onion, finely
chopped
100 g lean lamb mince
^{1}/2 teaspoon ground
allspice
^{1}/2 teaspoon ground
cinnamon
^{1}/3 cup (80 ml) beef stock
2 tablespoons pine nuts
2 tablespoons chopped
fresh mint
oil, for deep-frying

Kibbeh

1. Cover the wheat with boiling water and leave for 5 minutes. Drain in a colander, pressing well to remove the water. Spread on paper towels to absorb any moisture.
2. Process the wheat, lamb, onion, flour and allspice until a fine paste forms. Season well. Refrigerate for 1 hour.
3. To make the filling, heat the oil in a frying pan, add the onion and cook over low heat for 3 minutes, or until soft. Add the mince, allspice and cinnamon, and cook, stirring, over high heat, for 3 minutes. Add the stock and cook, partially covered, over low heat for 6 minutes, or until the mince is soft. Roughly chop the pine nuts and stir in with the mint. Season well with salt and cracked pepper, then transfer to a bowl and allow to cool.

4. Shape 2 tablespoons of the wheat mixture into a sausage shape 6 cm long. Dip your hands in cold water, and, with your finger, make a long hole through the centre and gently work your finger around to make a shell. Fill with 2 teaspoons of the filling and seal, moulding it into a torpedo shape. Smooth over any cracks with your fingers. Place on a foil-lined tray and refrigerate, uncovered, for 1 hour.
5. Fill a deep pan one-third full of oil and heat until a cube of bread dropped into the oil browns in 15 seconds. Deep-fry the kibbeh in batches for 2–3 minutes, or until browned. Drain on paper towels. Serve hot.

NUTRITION PER SERVE
*Protein 4.5 g; Fat 3 g;
Carbohydrate 10 g; Dietary
Fibre 2 g; Cholesterol
6.5 mg; 350 kJ (85 cal)*

Spoon 2 teaspoons of the filling into the centre and close the open end.

Mould into a smooth torpedo shape with pointed ends.

Meatballs

Preparation time:
  25 minutes +
  30 minutes chilling
Total cooking time:
  20 minutes
Makes about 28

115 g (4 slices) white
  bread, crusts removed
150 g pork mince
150 g veal mince
1 tablespoon chopped
  fresh flat-leaf parsley
1 tablespoon chopped
  fresh mint
1 onion, grated
1/2 teaspoon ground
  cumin
1 egg
1/4 cup (25 g) grated
  kefalotyri or Parmesan
1/2 cup (60 g) plain
  flour
olive oil, for shallow-
  frying

1. Cover the bread
with water in a bowl,
and squeeze out as
much water as possible.
Place in a large bowl
with the mince, parsley,
mint, onion, cumin,
egg and cheese. Season.
Knead the mixture by
hand for 2–3 minutes
until smooth. Cover
and refrigerate for
30 minutes.
2. Put the flour in a
shallow dish. With
wet hands, roll level
tablespoons of mixture
into balls. Heat the
shallow-frying oil over
medium heat. Toss the
meatballs in the flour.
Shallow-fry in batches
for 3–5 minutes, or
until the meatballs are
browned and cooked
through. Drain on
paper towels. Serve hot.

NUTRITION PER MEATBALL
*Protein 3.5 g; Fat 2 g;
Carbohydrate 3.5 g; Dietary
Fibre 0 g; Cholesterol
10 mg; 195 kJ (45 cal)*

Mussels Saganaki

Preparation time:
  45 minutes
Total cooking time:
  25 minutes
Serves 6

750 g small black
  mussels
1/2 cup (125 ml) dry
  white wine
3 sprigs fresh thyme
1 bay leaf
1 tablespoon olive oil
1 large onion, finely
  chopped
1 clove garlic, finely
  chopped
420 g ripe tomatoes,
  halved, grated and
  skin discarded
2 tablespoons tomato
  paste
1/2 teaspoon sugar
1 tablespoon red wine
  vinegar
70 g feta, crumbled
1 teaspoon fresh thyme
  leaves

1. Scrub the mussels
and remove the beards.
Discard any open
mussels. Bring the wine,
thyme and bay leaf to
the boil in a large pan,
add the mussels and
cook for 5 minutes.
Pour the mussel liquid
through a strainer into
a heatproof jug and
reserve. Discard any
unopened mussels.
Remove one half shell
from each mussel and
discard.
2. Heat the oil in a pan,
add the onion and cook
over medium heat for
3 minutes. Add the garlic
and cook for 1 minute,
or until fragrant. Pour
in the reserved mussel
liquid, increase the heat
and bring it to the boil,
then boil for 2 minutes,
or until almost dry.
Add the tomatoes,
tomato paste and
sugar, then reduce the
heat and simmer for
5 minutes. Add the
vinegar and simmer
for 5 minutes.
3. Add the mussels
and cook over medium
heat for 1 minute, or
until heated through.
Top with the crumbled
feta and thyme leaves.
Serve hot.

NUTRITION PER SERVE
*Protein 5 g; Fat 9 g;
Carbohydrate 4 g; Dietary
Fibre 1.5 g; Cholesterol
10 mg; 891 kJ (210 cal)*

*Meatballs (top) and
Mussels Saganaki*

Felafel

Preparation time:
  20 minutes
  + overnight soaking
  + 2 hours chilling
Total cooking time:
  15 minutes
Makes about 16

250 g dried chickpeas
4 spring onions, chopped
2 cloves garlic, crushed
1/2 cup (15 g) chopped
  fresh flat-leaf parsley
1/4 cup (15 g) chopped
  fresh mint
1/2 cup (25 g) chopped
  fresh coriander
1/4 teaspoon cayenne
  pepper
2 teaspoons ground
  cumin
2 teaspoons ground
  coriander
1/2 teaspoon baking
  powder
oil, for deep-frying

1. Cover the chickpeas with plenty of cold water and leave overnight. Drain well.
2. Combine the chickpeas, spring onions, garlic, parsley, mint, coriander, cayenne pepper, cumin, ground coriander, baking powder and 1 teaspoon salt. Process in batches for 30–40 seconds, or until finely chopped and the mixture is

sticky and holds together. Refrigerate, uncovered, for at least 2 hours.
3. Press 2 tablespoons of mixture together in the palm of your hand and form into a patty. Fill a deep pan one-third full of oil and heat until a cube of bread dropped into the oil browns in 15 seconds. Deep-fry the felafel in batches for 3–4 minutes, or until well browned. Drain on paper towels and serve hot with hummus (see page 49).

NUTRITION PER FELAFEL
Protein 3 g; Fat 3.5 g; Carbohydrate 6 g; Dietary Fibre 2 g; Cholesterol 0 mg; 265 kJ (65 cal)

Labneh

Preparation time:
  20 minutes +
  4 days chilling
Total cooking time:
  Nil
Makes 12

2 cups (500 g) thick
  Greek-style yoghurt
2 teaspoons sea salt
1 tablespoon dried
  oregano
2 teaspoons dried
  thyme leaves
1 bay leaf
1 1/3 cups (350 ml)
  olive oil

1. Fold a 60 cm x 30 cm piece of muslin in half to make a 30 cm square.
2. Combine the yoghurt, salt and 1 teaspoon black pepper in a bowl. Line a bowl with the muslin and spoon the mixture into the centre. Bring the corners together and, using a piece of kitchen string, tie as closely as possible to the yoghurt, leaving a loop at the end. Thread the loop through the handle of a wooden spoon and hang over a bowl to drain in the refrigerator for 3 days.
3. Combine the oregano and thyme in a shallow bowl. Pour half the oil into a 2 cup (500 ml) jar and add the bay leaf.
4. Roll level tablespoons of the mixture into balls. Toss in the combined herbs and place into the jar of oil. Pour in the remaining oil to cover the balls completely, seal and refrigerate for at least 1 day. Serve at room temperature.

NUTRITION PER LABNEH
Protein 2 g; Fat 6 g; Carbohydrate 2 g; Dietary Fibre 0 g; Cholesterol 3 mg; 240 kJ (57 cal)

Note: Labneh can be made up to 2 months ahead and kept in the refrigerator. The oil will turn white and set in the refrigerator, but will return to liquid at room temperature.

Felafel (top) with Labneh

Chorizo salad with mint

Preparation time:
  30 minutes
Total cooking time:
  25 minutes
Serves 6

5 chorizo sausages
^{1}/2 cup (125 ml) red
  wine vinegar
3 tablespoons caster
  sugar
1 large red onion,
  thinly sliced
1 tablespoon shredded
  fresh mint

1. Preheat the oven
to moderate 180°C
(350°F/Gas 4).
2. Prick the chorizo
sausages with a fork
and roast in the oven
for 10–20 minutes, or
until cooked through.
Set aside to cool.
3. In a large pan with
a tight-fitting lid,
combine the red wine
vinegar and the sugar.
Stir over low heat until
the sugar dissolves.
Add the onion, cover,
and cook over low
heat for 2 minutes.
Remove from the heat
and allow to cool.
Drain, reserving ^{1}/4 cup
(60 ml) of the cooking
liquid.
4. Slice the chorizo
sausage into bite-sized
slices and toss in a
bowl with the drained
onions and shredded

mint. Serve warm or
cold, drizzled with the
reserved liquid.

NUTRITION PER SERVE
*Protein 8 g; Fat 15 g;
Carbohydrate 5.5 g; Dietary
Fibre 0.5 g; Cholesterol
40 mg; 940 kJ (225 cal)*

Barbecued quail

Preparation time:
  40 minutes +
  3 hours chilling
Total cooking time:
  10 minutes
Serves 6

6 quail
1 cup (250 ml) dry red
  wine
2 sticks celery, including
  tops, chopped
1 carrot, chopped
1 small onion, chopped
1 bay leaf, torn into
  small pieces
1 teaspoon allspice
1 teaspoon dried thyme
2 cloves garlic, crushed
2 tablespoons olive oil
2 tablespoons lemon
  juice
1 lemon, cut into
  wedges for serving

1. To prepare the quail,
use poultry shears to
cut down either side
of the backbone, then
discard the backbone.
Remove the innards,
wash the inside of the
quail and pat dry with

paper towels. Place the
quail breast-side-up
on the bench, open out
flat and gently press to
flatten. Using poultry
shears, cut in half
through the breast then
cut each half in half
again into the thigh and
drumstick piece and
breast and wing piece.
2. In a non-metallic
bowl, combine the
wine, celery, carrot,
onion, bay leaf and
allspice. Add the quail
and stir to coat. Cover
and refrigerate for
3 hours, or preferably
overnight, stirring
occasionally. Drain and
sprinkle with thyme,
salt and pepper.
3. Whisk the garlic,
oil and lemon juice in
a small bowl.
4. Heat a lightly oiled
barbecue plate until hot
or heat a grill to its
highest setting. Reduce
the heat to medium and
cook the quail breast
pieces for 4–5 minutes
on each side and the
drumstick pieces for
3 minutes each side,
or until tender and
cooked through.
Brush frequently with
the lemon mixture.
Serve hot with lemon.

NUTRITION PER SERVE
*Protein 7 g; Fat 12.5 g;
Carbohydrate 2 g; Dietary
Fibre 1 g; Cholesterol
0 mg; 1150 kJ (275 cal)*

*Chorizo salad with mint (top) and
Barbecued quail*

Put the cod in a large bowl, cover with water and soak for 8–12 hours.

When the fish is cool enough to handle, remove the skin and bones.

Bacalao croquettes with skordalia

Preparation time:
  50 minutes +
  8–12 hours soaking
Total cooking time:
  55 minutes
Makes 24

400 g dried salt cod or
  bacalao (see Note)
300 g floury potatoes,
  unpeeled
1 small (25 g) brown
  pickling onion,
  grated
2 tablespoons chopped
  fresh flat-leaf parsley
1 egg, lightly beaten
oil, for deep-frying

Skordalia
250 g floury potatoes,
  unpeeled
2 cloves garlic, crushed
1 tablespoon white
  wine vinegar
2 tablespoons olive
  oil

1. Soak the cod in a large bowl covered with water for 8–12 hours, changing the water three times. This will remove the excess salt from the cod. Drain on paper towels.

2. To make the skordalia, boil or steam the potatoes until tender, remove the peel and mash. Allow to cool and add the garlic, vinegar and oil. Season with salt and cracked black pepper, then mix with a fork. Set aside.

3. Put the cod in a pan, cover with water, bring to the boil and cook for 15 minutes. Drain well and dry on paper towels. When cool enough to handle, remove the skin and bones from the cod and flake with your fingers into a bowl. Meanwhile, boil or steam the potatoes until tender, remove the peel and mash.

4. Add the mashed potato to the cod with the onion, parsley, egg and 1/2 teaspoon cracked pepper. Mix well with a wooden spoon to form a thick mixture. Taste before seasoning with salt.

5. Fill a deep pan one-third full of oil and heat until a cube of bread dropped into the oil browns in 15 seconds. Drop level tablespoons of the mixture into the oil and cook in batches for 2–3 minutes, or until well browned. Drain. Serve hot with skordalia.

NUTRITION PER SERVE
Protein 5 g; Fat 4 g; Carbohydrate 3.5 g; Dietary Fibre 1 g; Cholesterol 75 mg; 365 kJ (85 cal)

Note: Dried bacalao or salted cod is available at delicatessens or fish markets. The skordalia can be made up to 4 days ahead and kept covered in the refrigerator until needed.

Bacalao croquettes with skordalia

Use your fingers to flake the cod into a bowl and set aside.

Drop level tablespoons of the mixture into the hot oil and cook until browned.

Chicken rolls

Preparation time:
  1 hour 15 minutes
Total cooking time:
  1 hour 5 minutes
Makes about 40

60 g butter
1 large onion, chopped
2 cloves garlic, crushed
2 tablespoons plain
  flour
$1/2$ cup (125 ml)
  chicken stock
$1/2$ cup (125 ml) milk
1 large barbecued
  chicken, skin removed
  and flesh shredded
$1/4$ cup (25 g) grated
  Parmesan
2 teaspoons fresh
  thyme leaves
$1/4$ cup (25 g) dry
  breadcrumbs
2 eggs, lightly beaten
13 sheets filo pastry,
  cut into thirds
  crossways
140 g butter, extra,
  melted

1. Melt the butter in a
pan and add the onion.
Cook over low heat for
12 minutes, or until soft,
stirring occasionally.
Increase the heat to
medium–high and add
the garlic. Cook, stirring
for 1 minute, then
add the flour and stir
over heat for a further
1 minute. Remove from
the heat and gradually
add the stock and milk,
stirring constantly until
smooth. Return to high
heat and bring to the
boil, stirring constantly
until the sauce boils
and thickens. Boil for
1 minute, then remove
from the heat and add
the chicken, Parmesan,
thyme, breadcrumbs,
salt and pepper. Cool,
then stir in the eggs.
2. Preheat the oven
to hot 220°C (425°F/
Gas 7). Lightly grease
three baking trays.
3. Put one piece of filo
pastry on the bench
with the short end
closest to you (cover
the remaining pieces
with a damp tea towel).
Brush with the extra
melted butter and place
a level tablespoon of
chicken mixture on the
base end closest to you.
Fold in the sides, brush
along the length with
butter and roll up
tightly to form a roll
7–8 cm long. Put onto
the baking tray and
brush the top with
some of the butter.
Repeat with the
remaining filo, butter
and chicken mixture.
4. Bake for 15 minutes
in the top half of the
oven until well
browned. Serve hot.

NUTRITION PER ROLL
*Protein 4 g; Fat 5.5 g;
Carbohydrate 3 g; Dietary
Fibre 0 g; Cholesterol
35 mg; 335 kJ (80 cal)*

Pickled baby cos

Preparation time:
  20 minutes + cooling
Total cooking time:
  5 minutes
Serves 6

$1/4$ cup (60 ml)
  balsamic vinegar
$1/4$ cup (60 ml) olive oil
1 teaspoon soft brown
  sugar
3 baby cos (see Note)

1. In a bowl combine the
vinegar, oil and sugar.
2. Peel off the outer
layers of lettuce to
reach the heart of each
cos. Wash thoroughly
under running water.
Cut the hearts in half.
3. Put the cos hearts in
a pan of lightly salted
boiling water, and
simmer for 3 minutes,
or until just tender but
still in one piece. Drain.
Place in a shallow dish,
top with the balsamic
mixture, and allow to
cool before serving.

NUTRITION PER SERVE
*Protein 0 g; Fat 10 g;
Carbohydrate 1 g; Dietary
Fibre 0.5 g; Cholesterol
0 mg; 380 kJ (90 cal)*

Note: If unavailable,
choose firm medium-
sized cos. Remove
about half of the outer
leaves to find the heart.

*Chicken rolls (top)
with Pickled baby cos*

Tomato and eggplant borek

Preparation time:
50 minutes + 1 hour
refrigeration
Total cooking time:
1 hour
Makes 30

75 g butter, melted
1/3 cup (80 ml) olive oil
11/2 cups (185 g) plain
  flour

Filling
250 g tomatoes
2 teaspoons olive oil
1 small onion, chopped
1/2 teaspoon ground
  cumin
300 g eggplant, cut into
  2 cm cubes
2 teaspoons tomato
  paste
1 tablespoon chopped
  fresh coriander
1 egg, lightly beaten

1. Put the butter, oil
and 1/3 cup (80 ml)
water into a bowl.
Season well with salt.
Gradually add the flour
in batches, mixing with
a wooden spoon, to
form an oily, lumpy
dough that leaves the
side of the bowl.
Knead gently to bring
the dough together,
cover with plastic wrap
and refrigerate for
1 hour.

2. Core the tomatoes
and cut a small cross at
the base. Plunge into a
pan of boiling water
and leave for 1 minute.
Drain, plunge into cold
water, then remove the
peel. Halve the tomatoes,
squeeze over a bowl to
remove the seeds, and
finely chop the flesh.
3. Heat the oil in a
frying pan, add the
onion and cook, stirring,
over low heat for
2–3 minutes, or until
soft. Add the cumin,
cook for 1 minute, then
add the eggplant and
cook, stirring, for
8–10 minutes, or until
the eggplant begins
to soften. Stir in the
tomato and paste. Cook
over medium heat for
15 minutes, or until the
mixture becomes dry.
Stir occasionally.
Season and stir in the
coriander. Cool.
4. Preheat the oven
to moderate 180°C
(350°F/Gas 4). Lightly
grease two oven trays.
5. Roll out half the
pastry on a lightly
floured surface until
2 mm thick. Using an
81/2 cm cutter, cut
rounds from the pastry.
Spoon 2 level teaspoons
of the mixture into the
centre of each round,
lightly brush the edges
with water, and fold
over the filling,

expelling any air. Press
firmly and crimp the
edge with a fork to seal.
Place on the oven trays
and brush with the
beaten egg. Bake in the
top half of the oven for
25 minutes, or until
browned and crisp.

NUTRITION PER BOREK
*Protein 1 g; Fat 5 g;
Carbohydrate 5 g; Dietary
Fibre 0.5 g; Cholesterol
12 mg; 295 kJ (70 cal)*

Greek village salad

Preparation time:
20 minutes
Total cooking time: Nil
Serves 6–8

6 tomatoes, cut into
  thin wedges
1 red onion, cut into
  thin rings
2 Lebanese cucumbers,
  sliced.
185 g Kalamata olives
200 g feta
1/2 cup (125 ml) extra
  virgin olive oil
dried oregano, to garnish

1. Combine the tomato,
onion, cucumber and
olives in a bowl. Season
to taste.
2. Break the feta into
large pieces and scatter
over the top. Top with
olive oil and oregano.

NUTRITION PER SERVE (8)
*Protein 6.5 g; Fat 20 g;
Carbohydrate 4 g; Dietary
Fibre 2.5 g; Cholesterol
17 mg; 980 kJ (235 cal)*

*Tomato and eggplant borek (top)
with Greek village salad*

Spinach pie

Preparation time:
  50 minutes + 1 hour
  chilling
Total cooking time:
  50 minutes
Makes 16 pieces

2 cups (250 g) plain
  flour
30 g butter, chopped
¹/4 cup (60 ml) olive oil
¹/2 cup (125 ml) warm
  water

Filling
420 g English spinach
1 leek, white part only,
  halved lengthways
  and thinly sliced
¹/4 teaspoon ground
  nutmeg
2 teaspoons chopped
  fresh dill
200 g feta, crumbled
1 tablespoon dry
  breadcrumbs
3 eggs, lightly beaten
2 tablespoons olive
  oil

1. Lightly oil a 28 cm
x 18 cm x 3 cm tin.
2. Sift the flour into
a bowl and stir in
¹/2 teaspoon salt.
Using your fingertips,
rub the butter into
the flour until the
mixture resembles fine
breadcrumbs. Pour in
the oil and rub it in by
lifting the flour mixture
onto one hand and
lightly rubbing the
other hand over the top.

The mixture should
clump together. Make a
well in the centre and,
while mixing by hand,
add enough water to
form a firm supple
dough. Knead gently
to bring the dough
together—it may not
be completely smooth.
Cover with plastic wrap
and chill for 1 hour.
3. Trim the bottom
quarter from the
spinach stalks.
Wash and shred the
remaining leaves and
stalks. Pile the spinach
onto a clean tea towel,
twist as tightly as
possible and squeeze
dry. Put into a bowl
with the leek, nutmeg,
dill, feta, breadcrumbs
and ¹/2 teaspoon
cracked black pepper.
4. Preheat the oven to
hot 220°C (425°F/
Gas 7). Roll out just
over half the dough on
a lightly floured surface
until large enough to
line the base and sides
of the tin. Lift the
dough into the tin,
pressing evenly over the
base and sides.
5. Add the eggs and oil
to the spinach mixture.
Mix with your hand,
but do not overmix or
the mixture will become
too wet. Spoon into
the pastry-lined tin.
6. Roll out the
remaining pastry on a
lightly floured surface

until large enough to
cover the tin. Lift
onto the tin and press
the two pastry edges
firmly together to seal.
Trim the excess pastry
with a sharp knife
from the outer edge of
the tin, then brush the
top with a little extra
olive oil. Using a sharp
knife, mark into three
strips lengthways and
then diagonally into
diamonds. Make two
or three small slits
through the top layer
of pastry to allow the
steam to escape.
7. Bake the pie for
45–50 minutes in the
centre of the oven, or
until well browned.
Cover with foil if the
pastry is overbrowning.
The pie is cooked if it
slides when you gently
shake the tin. Turn
out onto wire rack to
cool for 10 minutes,
then turn onto a cutting
board or back into tin
to cut into diamonds.
Delicious served warm
or cold.

NUTRITION PER PIECE
*Protein 6 g; Fat 12 g;
Carbohydrate 12 g; Dietary
Fibre 1.5 g; Cholesterol
45 mg; 735 kJ (175 cal)*

Note: The pastry is even
better if it is made the
night before. White
spots on the surface of
the pastry are the oil
setting when cold.

Spinach pie

Meat patties with haloumi filling

Preparation time:
25 minutes +
30 minutes chilling
Total cooking time:
10 minutes
Makes 12

4 slices (125 g) white
  bread, crusts removed
350 g lamb or beef
  mince
2 teaspoons chopped
  fresh flat-leaf parsley
1 1/2 tablespoons
  chopped fresh mint
1 small onion, grated
1 egg, lightly beaten
70 g haloumi (see Note)
2 tablespoons plain
  flour
olive oil, for shallow-
  frying

1. Put the bread in a
bowl, cover with water
and then squeeze out as
much water as possible.
Place the bread in a
bowl with the mince,
parsley, mint, onion,
egg, pepper and
1/2 teaspoon salt.
Knead the mixture by
hand for 2–3 minutes,
breaking up the mince
and any large pieces of
bread with your fingers.
The mixture should
be smooth and leave
the side of the bowl.
Cover and refrigerate

for 30 minutes.
2. Cut the haloumi into
12 rectangular pieces,
3 cm x 1 cm x 1 cm.
Place the flour in a
shallow dish. Divide the
mince mixture into level
tablespoon portions.
Roll a portion into a
long shape and flatten
in the palm of your
hand. Place the cheese
in the centre and top
with another portion of
mince. Pinch the edges
together and roll into a
torpedo shape 6–7 cm
long. Repeat with the
remaining mince.
3. Heat the oil in a
deep frying pan until a
cube of bread dropped
into the oil browns in
15 seconds. Toss half
the meat patties in the
flour, shake off the
excess flour and fry
for 3–5 minutes, or
until browned all over
and cooked through.
Drain well on paper
towels and repeat with
the remaining meat
patties. Serve hot.

NUTRITION PER SERVE
*Protein 9 g; Fat 8.5 g;
Carbohydrate 6.5 g; Dietary
Fibre 0.5 g; Cholesterol
50 mg; 580 kJ (140 cal)*

Note: Haloumi is a
creamy white sheep's
milk cheese kept in a
brine. It can be bought
from delicatessens and
supermarkets.

*Meat patties with haloumi filling (top)
with Tabbouleh*

Tabbouleh

Preparation time:
10 minutes +
30 minutes standing
Total cooking time:
Nil
Serves 4

3/4 cup (130 g) burghul
2 tomatoes, chopped
4 spring onions, finely
  chopped
1 yellow capsicum,
  finely chopped
1 1/2 cups (45 g) chopped
  fresh flat-leaf parsley
1/4 cup (15 g) chopped
  fresh mint
1/4 cup (60 ml) olive oil
1/4 cup (60 ml) lemon
  juice
1 clove garlic, crushed

1. Cover the burghul
with 3/4 cup (185 ml)
boiling water. Leave for
30 minutes, or until the
water is absorbed and
the grains have swollen.
2. Combine the tomato,
spring onion, capsicum,
parsley, mint and burghul
in a bowl. Season well.
3. Whisk together the
oil, juice and garlic.
Pour over the salad,
toss and serve cold.

NUTRITION PER SERVE
*Protein 5 g; Fat 15 g;
Carbohydrate 20 g; Dietary
Fibre 7 g; Cholesterol
0 mg; 1025 kJ (245 cal)*

Note: Burghul is cracked
wheat, also known as
bulgar wheat.

Marinated Olives

To ensure the olives store well, sterilise the jar first by rinsing it with boiling water, then place it in a warm oven until it is completely dry. For best results, these olives should be served at room temperature.

LEMON, GARLIC AND THYME

Cut 8 thin slices of lemon into quarters and put in a bowl with $1^{1}/_{2}$ teaspoons dried thyme leaves, 2 well-bruised cloves garlic, 250 g Kalamata olives and 250 g green olives. Spoon into a 1-litre sterilised jar with a lid and pour in about $1^{3}/_{4}$ cups (440 ml) olive oil, or enough to cover the olives completely. Seal and refrigerate for up to 3 months. Ready to eat in 2 days.

CHILLI, HERB AND LEMON

Combine 500 g cured black olives (these are the olives with a wrinkled appearance) with 2 teaspoons finely grated lemon rind, 2 teaspoons fresh oregano and 3 teaspoons dried chilli flakes. Transfer to a 3-cup (750 ml) sterilised jar with a lid and cover with olive oil. Seal and refrigerate for up to 3 months. Ready to eat after 2 days.

DILL, GARLIC AND ORANGE

In a bowl, combine 500 g Kalamata olives with 3 tablespoons coarsely chopped fresh dill, 1 bruised clove garlic, 4 thin slices of orange cut into eighths and 2 torn bay leaves. Spoon into a 1-litre sterilised jar with a lid and pour in about $1^{3}/_{4}$ cups (440 ml) olive oil or enough to cover the olives completely. Seal and refrigerate for up to 3 months. Ready to eat in 2 days.

From left to right: Coriander and orange; Chilli, herb and lemon; Lemon, garlic and thyme; Mixed olive pickles; 'A Sevilla'; Dill, garlic and orange.

MIXED OLIVE PICKLES

Combine 200 g jumbo green olives, 4 thickly sliced gherkins, 1 tablespoon capers, 2 quartered brown pickled onions, 2 teaspoons mustard seeds and 1 tablespoon fresh dill sprigs in a bowl. Spoon into a 2-cup (500 ml) sterilised jar with a lid and pour in 1/2 cup (125 ml) tarragon vinegar. Top with about 1/2 cup (125 ml) olive oil, or enough to cover completely. Seal and refrigerate for up to 3 months. Ready to eat after 2 days. Shake the jar occasionally.

'A SEVILLA'

Combine 1 tablespoon fresh rosemary leaves, 1 teaspoon dried thyme leaves, 1 torn bay leaf, 1 teaspoon lightly crushed fennel seeds, 2 well-bruised cloves garlic, 3 chopped anchovy fillets and 500 g stuffed green olives in a bowl. Spoon into a 1-litre sterilised jar with a lid and pour in 1/2 cup (125 ml) tarragon vinegar. Top with about 3/4 cup (185 ml) olive oil, or enough to completely. cover. Seal and refrigerate for up to 3 months. Ready to eat after 2 days. Shake the jar occasionally.

CORIANDER AND ORANGE

Lightly crush 2 teaspoons coriander seeds with a mortar and pestle. Combine the crushed coriander seeds, 1 teaspoon cumin seeds and 2 teaspoons grated orange rind in a bowl. Add 500 g jumbo green olives and mix together well. Spoon into a sterilised 1-litre jar with lid and pour in about 1 3/4 cups (440 ml) olive oil, or enough to completely cover the olives. Seal the jar and refrigerate for up to 3 months. Ready to eat after 2 days.

Baked sardines

Preparation time:
  30 minutes
Total cooking time:
  20 minutes
Serves 6

6 fresh whole sardines
1/4 cup (60 ml) olive oil
2 tablespoons lemon
  juice
1 small clove garlic,
  chopped
1 1/2 teaspoons dried
  oregano

1. Preheat the oven
to hot 210°C (415°F/
Gas 6–7). Clean the
sardines by scraping a
small knife along the
body of the sardine,
starting from the tail
end to remove any
scales (this is best done
under running water).
Make a slit along the
gut. Cut the head and
pull away slowly—the
intestines should come
away with the head.
Open the gut cavity and
clean away remaining
intestines. Pat dry and
drain on paper towels.
2. Put the sardines into
an ovenproof dish large
enough to fit them
snuggly in one layer
and season with salt
and 1/2 teaspoon pepper.
Drizzle with oil and
lemon juice and sprinkle
with garlic and oregano.
Turn to coat and bake,
uncovered, in the top

half of the oven for
15–20 minutes, or until
the flesh flakes and
starts to come away
from the bone. Serve hot
or warm.

NUTRITION PER SERVE
*Protein 2.5 g; Fat 10 g;
Carbohydrate 0.5 g; Dietary
Fibre 0 g; Cholesterol
15 mg; 115 kJ (48 cal)*

Beetroot with skordalia

Preparation time:
  25 minutes
Total cooking time:
  1 hour
Serves 6–8

Skordalia
250 g floury potatoes,
  unpeeled
2 cloves garlic, crushed
1 tablespoon white
  wine vinegar
2 tablespoons olive oil

1 kg beetroot, including
  leaves
1/4 cup (60 ml) extra
  virgin olive oil
1 tablespoon red wine
  vinegar

1. Boil or steam the
potatoes until tender,
remove the peel and
mash. Cool, then mash
with the garlic, vinegar
and oil. Season well.
2. Cut the stems with
leaves from the beetroot

bulbs, leaving a 2 cm
stalk, and trim any
tough tops off the leaves.
Cut the whole leaf and
stem length into smaller
sections (halves or
thirds), and wash well.
3. Brush the bulbs to
remove any dirt. Bring
a large pan of water
to the boil, add the
unpeeled bulbs and
cook over high heat
for 20–40 minutes
(depending on bulb size),
or until tender when
pierced with a sharp
knife. Remove from the
pan with a slotted
spoon and cool slightly.
4. Return the cooking
water to the boil,
adding more water
if necessary. Add the
leaves and stems, and
boil for 8 minutes, or
until tender. Turn once
during cooking. Drain.
5. Put on a pair of
rubber gloves and peel
the skin from the bulbs.
Cut in half and then
into thick slices.
6. Arrange the leaves
and sliced bulbs on a
serving plate. Combine
the oil and vinegar and
season to taste. Drizzle
over the leaves and
bulbs, and serve the
skordalia on the side.

NUTRITION PER SERVE (8)
*Protein 3 g; Fat 12 g;
Carbohydrate 15 g; Dietary
Fibre 4.5 g; Cholesterol
0 mg; 746 kJ (178 cal)*

*Baked sardines (top)
with Beetroot with skordalia*

Lamb's liver with lemon

Preparation time:
15 minutes
Total cooking time:
10 minutes
Serves 6–8

500 g lamb's liver
1/4 cup (30 g) plain
 flour
1/2 teaspoon paprika
2 tablespoons olive oil
2 tablespoons lemon
 juice
1 teaspoon dried
 oregano

1. Wash the liver thoroughly, trim off any fatty deposits and cut into 2 cm thick slices. Cut the larger slices of liver in half or into thirds.
2. In a shallow dish, combine the flour and paprika and season with 1/2 teaspoon each of salt and cracked black pepper. Heat the oil in a frying pan over medium heat. Toss a third of the livers in the seasoned flour, shake off the excess flour and fry for 1 minute on each side or until browned, crusty and still pink inside. Drain on paper towels and place on warmed serving plate.

Repeat with the remaining slices of liver, cooking them in two batches. Cover with foil to keep warm.
3. Remove the pan from the heat and add the lemon juice—it should bubble in the hot pan. Allow the bubbles to subside, then pour the pan juices over the livers and sprinkle with oregano. Serve hot.

NUTRITION PER SERVE (8)
Protein 15 g; Fat 9.5 g; Carbohydrate 4.5 g; Dietary Fibre 0 g; Cholesterol 270 mg; 660 kJ (160 cal)

Eggplant salad

Preparation time:
30 minutes +
1 hour chilling
Total cooking time:
1 hour
Serves 4–6

1 red capsicum
1 large eggplant, cut
 into four wedges
1/2 red onion, cut into
 thin wedges
1 medium tomato,
 chopped
1 tablespoon chopped
 fresh flat-leaf parsley
1 small clove garlic,
 crushed
3 teaspoons extra
 virgin olive oil
1 teaspoon red wine
 vinegar

1. Preheat the oven to moderately hot 200°C (400°F/Gas 6) and line a baking tray with foil.
2. Cut the capsicum into quarters and remove the seeds and the membrane. Place the capsicum skin-side-up and the eggplant on the baking tray. Bake for 50–60 minutes, or until the capsicum skin has blistered and the eggplant is browned and soft when pierced with a sharp knife.
3. Leave until cool enough to handle, then carefully remove the skins from both vegetables. Cut the capsicum into long thin strips and roughly chop the eggplant flesh. Place in a bowl with the onion, tomato, parsley and garlic. Whisk together the oil and vinegar in a small jug, and season with plenty of salt and cracked black pepper. Pour over the salad and mix well. Cover and refrigerate for 1 hour before serving.

NUTRITION PER SERVE (6)
Protein 1.5 g; Fat 2.5 g; Carbohydrate 2.5 g; Dietary Fibre 2 g; Cholesterol 0 mg; 170 kJ (40 cal)

Note: This recipe can be made a day ahead and stored in an airtight container in the refrigerator.

Lamb's liver with lemon (top)
with Eggplant salad

Fried whitebait

Preparation time:
10 minutes
Total cooking time:
10 minutes
Serves 6

500 g whitebait
2 teaspoons sea salt
1/3 cup (40 g) plain
flour
1/4 cup (30 g) cornflour
2 teaspoons finely
chopped fresh flat-leaf
parsley
oil, for deep-frying
1 lemon, cut into
wedges, for serving

1. Combine the white-bait and sea salt in a bowl and mix well. Cover and refrigerate.
2. Combine the sifted flours and parsley in a bowl and season well with cracked pepper. Fill a deep heavy-based pan one-third full of oil and heat until a cube of bread dropped into the oil browns in 15 seconds. Toss a third of the whitebait in the flour mixture, shake off the excess flour, and deep-fry for 1 1/2 minutes, or until pale and crisp. Drain well on crumpled paper towels. Repeat with the remaining whitebait, cooking in two batches.
3. Reheat the oil and fry the whitebait a second

time in three batches for 1 minute each, or until lightly browned. Drain on paper towels and serve hot with lemon wedges.

NUTRITION PER SERVE
*Protein 20 g; Fat 9 g;
Carbohydrate 9.5 g; Dietary
Fibre 0.5 g; Cholesterol
60 mg; 795 kJ (190 cal)*

Deep-fried squid

Preparation time:
30 minutes +
30 minutes chilling
Total cooking time:
5 minutes
Serves 4

480 g (about 18)
small squid
1/3 cup (40 g) plain
flour
oil, for deep-frying
1/2 lemon, cut into
wedges, for serving

1. To clean the squid, gently pull the tentacles away from the hood—the intestines should come away with them. Remove the intestines from the tentacles by cutting under the eyes and remove the beak if it remains in the centre of the tentacles. Pull away the soft bone from the hood. Rub the hoods under running water and the skin

should come away easily. Wash the hoods and tentacles and drain well. Place in a bowl and season well with salt. Cover and refrigerate for about 30 minutes.
2. Combine the flour with a pinch each of salt and cracked pepper in a shallow dish. Fill a deep heavy-based pan one-third full of oil and heat until a cube of bread dropped into the oil browns in 15 seconds. Coat the calamari hoods in flour and deep-fry in batches for about 30–60 seconds, or until lightly browned and tender. Toss the tentacles in the flour and deep-fry for 20–30 seconds, or until lightly browned and tender. Partially cover the deep-fryer while cooking as the squid tends to splatter. Drain on paper towels then transfer to a serving platter, sprinkle with salt and serve hot with lemon wedges.

NUTRITION PER SERVE
*Protein 20 g; Fat 11 g;
Carbohydrate 7.5 g; Dietary
Fibre 0.5 g; Cholesterol
240 mg; 905 kJ (215 cal)*

Note: Cleaned squid are sometimes available from fishmongers.

*Fried whitebait (top)
with Deep-fried squid*

Remove the eyes by cutting a round of flesh from the base of the head.

Carefully slit open the head and remove the gut.

Octopus in red wine

Preparation time:
45 minutes
Total cooking time:
2 hours 20 minutes
Serves 4

1 kg small octopus
2 tablespoons olive oil
180 g small brown
  pickling onions
$1/3$ cup (80 ml) red wine
  vinegar
$3/4$ cup (185 ml) dry red
  wine
1 ripe tomato, halved,
  grated and skin
  discarded
1 bay leaf
1 teaspoon dried
  oregano leaves

1. To clean the octopus, use a small sharp knife and remove the head from the tentacles. Remove the eyes by cutting a round of flesh from the base of the head. To clean the head, carefully slit open the head and remove the gut. Cut the head in half. Push out the beak from the centre of the tentacles. Cut the tentacles into sets of four or two, depending on the size of the octopus. Pull away the skin from the head and tentacles if it comes away easily.

2. Place the octopus in a large pan and cook over high heat in its own liquid for 15–20 minutes, or until dry. Add the oil and the onions, and toss over heat until well coated. Add the vinegar, wine, tomato, bay leaf, oregano, 1 cup (250 ml) water and $1/2$ teaspoon cracked black pepper and bring to the boil. Reduce the heat to low and simmer for 1$1/2$ to 2 hours, or until the octopus is tender. If the octopus is not yet tender, add a little more water and continue cooking. The liquid remaining in the pan should just coat the octopus like a sauce. Delicious served hot with crusty bread.

NUTRITION PER SERVE
Protein 42 g; Fat 13 g; Carbohydrate 6.5 g; Dietary Fibre 1 g; Cholesterol 498 mg; 1314 kJ (315 cal)

Note: When choosing octopus, select those that are younger and smaller, as they will be more tender than the larger ones.
Variation: The octopus is closely related to squid and cuttlefish, so if you are unable to buy small octopus, either of these can be substituted.
Hint: Choose a ripe, but still firm, tomato to make grating easier.

Octopus in red wine

Use your fingers to push out the beak from the centre of the tentacles.

Cook the octopus in its own liquid over high heat until dry.

Pan-fried cheese

Preparation time:
  10 minutes
Total cooking time:
  5 minutes
Serves 2–3

250 g kefalograviera
  (see Note)
2 tablespoons plain
  flour
1/4 cup (60 ml) olive
  oil
1/2 teaspoon dried
  oregano
1/2 lemon cut into
  wedges, for serving

1. Cut the cheese into
1 cm slices. The pieces
can be as large as you
wish, as they can be cut
smaller for serving.
2. Put the flour in a
shallow dish and
season well with
cracked pepper. Toss
the cheese in the flour.
3. Heat the oil over
high heat in a frying
pan until hot. Add the
cheese to the pan and
cook for 1 minute,
or until browned and
crusty underneath.
Using an egg slice,
carefully turn the
cheese to brown the
other side. Lift onto
a serving plate and
sprinkle with oregano.
Serve hot with lemon
wedges, squeezing
lemon juice over the
top. Ideally served with
fresh bread.

Note: Kefalograviera
and kefalotyri are pale
hard sheep's milk cheeses
originating in Greece.

NUTRITION PER SERVE (3)
*Protein 35 g; Fat 45 g;
Carbohydrate 6 g; Dietary
Fibre 0.5 g; Cholesterol
80 mg; 2370 kJ (565 cal)*

Pickled octopus

Preparation time:
  30 minutes +
  1–2 days chilling
Total cooking time:
  1 hour
Serves 4–6

1 kg small octopus
12 whole black
  peppercorns
2 bay leaves
1 tablespoon fresh
  oregano
2 teaspoons fresh
  thyme
1 small clove garlic,
  thinly sliced
1 cup (250 ml) red
  wine vinegar
1 1/3 cups (350 ml)
  olive oil

1. To clean the octopus,
use a small sharp knife
and remove the head
from the tentacles.
Remove the eyes by
cutting a round of flesh
from the base of the
head. Carefully slit open
the head and remove
the gut. Cut the head in
half. Push out the beak
from the centre of the
tentacles. Cut the
tentacles into sets of
two. Pull away the
skin from the head and
tentacles if it comes
away easily.
2. Put the octopus,
peppercorns and bay
leaves in a pan and
cook, covered, over
medium–low heat in its
own liquid for 1 hour,
or until tender. Drain
and cool for 20 minutes.
Reserve the peppercorns
and bay leaves.
3. Sterilise a 1-litre
glass jar by rinsing with
boiling water and
drying in a warm oven.
Place the octopus,
peppercorns and bay
leaves into the jar.
Add the herbs and
garlic, and pour in the
vinegar and enough of
the oil to completely
cover the octopus, so
that it doesn't break the
surface. Seal and gently
shake the jar to mix
the ingredients.
4. Refrigerate for
1–2 days, shaking the
jar occasionally. Store
in the refrigerator for
up to 5 days. Return
to room temperature
before serving.

NUTRITION PER SERVE (6)
*Protein 30 g; Fat 15 g;
Carbohydrate 0 g; Dietary
Fibre 0 g; Cholesterol
330 mg; 1045 kJ (250 cal)*

*Pan-fried cheese (top)
with Pickled octopus*

Olive oil biscuits

Preparation time:
30 minutes +
1 hour 30 minutes
standing
Total cooking time:
1 hour 30 minutes
Makes about 45

7 g dried yeast
1 teaspoon sugar
1 1/2 cups (185 g) plain
  white flour
1 1/2 cups (225 g) plain
  wholemeal flour
1 teaspoon ground
  cinnamon
1 1/2 tablespoons
  sesame seeds, toasted
1/2 cup (125 ml) olive oil

Topping
4 ripe tomatoes, diced
160 g feta, crumbled
1/3 cup (80 ml) extra
  virgin olive oil
2 tablespoons red wine
  vinegar
1 teaspoon dried
  oregano

1. Combine the yeast, sugar, 2 tablespoons of the white flour and 1/4 cup (60 ml) warm water in a bowl. Cover with plastic wrap and leave in a warm place for 10 minutes, or until frothy.
2. Sift the remaining flours and cinnamon in a large bowl, return the husks to the bowl and stir through the sesame seeds and 1/2 teaspoon salt. Pour in the oil and rub it in by lifting the flour mixture onto one hand and lightly rubbing the other hand over the top. Make a well in the centre and add the yeast mixture and about 1/4 cup (60 ml) warm water, or enough to mix to a soft but not sticky dough.
3. Knead on a floured surface for about 2 minutes, or until smooth and elastic. Place in a lightly oiled bowl, turning the dough to coat in the oil. Cover loosely with plastic wrap and leave in a warm place for 45–60 minutes, or until doubled in bulk.
4. Lightly grease an oven tray. Punch down the dough and divide it into three portions and roll each on a lightly floured surface into a long sausage shape about 30 cm long. Place the first roll onto the tray. Cut through almost to the base of the roll at 2 cm intervals with a serrated knife (about 15 portions). Repeat with remaining rolls.
5. Cover with a tea towel and leave in a warm place for 30 minutes, or until well risen. Preheat the oven to moderately hot 200°C (400°F/Gas 6). Bake for 30 minutes, or until browned underneath and the rolls sound hollow when tapped. Reduce the temperature to very slow 120°C (250°F/Gas 1/2). Cool on the tray for 5 minutes.
6. Transfer each roll to a cutting board and cut through the markings. Place cut-side-up on two oven trays. Bake for 30 minutes, or until the top feels dry. Turn each biscuit and bake for a further 30 minutes, or until completely dry and crisp. Cool. Store in an airtight container for up to 3 weeks.
7. Dunk each biscuit quickly into cold water and place on a tray. Top with the combined tomato and feta. Drizzle on the combined oil and vinegar and sprinkle with oregano. Season.

NUTRITION PER SERVE
Protein 1.5 g; Fat 5.5 g; Carbohydrate 4 g; Dietary Fibre 0.5 g; Cholesterol 2.5 mg; 300 kJ (70 cal)

Variation: For a different topping, combine 10 pitted and quartered Kalamata olives, 1 sliced roasted capsicum and 2 tablespoons chopped flat-leaf parsley. Season. Drizzle on 3 tablespoons extra virgin olive oil and 1 tablespoon red wine vinegar, combined.

Olive oil biscuits

Barbecued haloumi

Preparation time:
  15 minutes
Total cooking time:
  10 minutes
Makes 10

1 French bread stick
250 g haloumi (see
  Note)
3 tablespoons olive oil
1 clove garlic, crushed
1/2 teaspoon finely
  chopped fresh mint

1. Cut the bread
diagonally into 1 1/2 cm
slices. Cut the haloumi
into the same number
of 3–5 mm thick slices
to fit the slice of bread.
2. Heat a lightly oiled
barbecue plate until
hot. Barbecue the bread
on both sides until well
browned and place
onto a serving plate.
Brush lightly with
1 tablespoon olive oil.
3. Brush the haloumi
with 1 tablespoon olive
oil and the garlic, and
barbecue for 1 minute
or until soft and
browned on both sides.
Lift with an egg slice
onto the bread, drizzle
with the remaining oil
and sprinkle with mint
and pepper. Serve hot.

NUTRITION PER PIECE
Protein 6.5 g; Fat 10 g;
Carbohydrate 7.5 g; Dietary
Fibre 0.5 g; Cholesterol
13 mg; 620 kJ (150 cal)

Note: Haloumi is a
creamy white sheep's
milk cheese kept in a
brine. It can be bought
in vacuum-packed
packets or in bulk from
delicatessens or most
supermarkets.

Lima bean casserole

Preparation time:
  20 minutes +
  overnight soaking
Total cooking time:
  2 hours
Serves 6–8

1 cup (185 g) dried
  lima beans
1/4 cup (60 ml) olive oil
1 large onion, halved
  and sliced
1 clove garlic, chopped
1 small carrot, chopped
1 small stick celery,
  chopped
400 g can crushed
  tomatoes
1 tablespoon tomato
  paste
2 teaspoons chopped
  fresh dill

1. Cover the lima beans
with plenty of cold
water and leave
overnight. Drain well.
2. Bring a large pan of
water to the boil, add
the beans and return
to the boil, then reduce
the heat to medium and

cook, partially covered,
for 45–60 minutes, or
until the beans are
tender but not mushy.
Drain. Preheat the oven
to moderate 180°C
(350°F/Gas 4).
3. Heat the oil in a
flameproof 2.5 litre
casserole over medium
heat. Add the onion,
garlic, carrot and
celery, and cook for
5 minutes, or until the
onion is translucent.
Add the crushed
tomatoes, tomato
paste and 1/2 cup
(125 ml) water. Bring
to the boil, then reduce
the heat and simmer
for 3 minutes.
4. Add the lima beans
and dill, and season to
taste with salt and
cracked pepper. Bring
back to the boil, then
transfer to the oven and
bake, uncovered, for
50 minutes, or until
thick and the beans are
soft. Serve hot or at
room temperature.

NUTRITION PER SERVE (8)
Protein 6 g; Fat 7.5 g;
Carbohydrate 10 g; Dietary
Fibre 5.5 g; Cholesterol
0 mg; 590 kJ (140 cal)

Note: Lima bean
casserole can be made
up to 3 days ahead and
kept covered in the
refrigerator. Return
to room temperature
before serving.

Barbecued haloumi (top)
with Lima bean casserole

Dips and Spreads

No meze feast would be complete without some of the delicious dips Mediterranean cuisine is famous for.

TARAMASALATA
Remove the crusts from 4 slices of white bread. Put the bread in a bowl, cover with water, drain and squeeze out as much water as possible, and place in a medium bowl. Finely grate a small onion into the bowl and add 100 g tarama (cod roe), 2 tablespoons freshly squeezed lemon juice, 3 tablespoons olive oil and a pinch of black pepper. Mix with a fork until well combined. Alternatively, process the ingredients until smooth. Can be made up to 3 days ahead and stored in an airtight container in the refrigerator. Makes about 1 cup (250 ml).

FETA SPREAD
Place 100 g ricotta, 175 g feta, 3 tablespoons olive oil, 3 teaspoons finely chopped fresh mint and $1/4$ teaspoon cracked black pepper in a bowl. Mix with a fork to mash the cheeses, yet still retain a lumpy texture. Can be made up to 3 days ahead and stored in an airtight container in the refrigerator. Makes about 1 cup (250 ml).

BABA GANOUJ
Make four shallow slits in a large (500 g) eggplant, then grill or barbecue for 15–20 minutes, turning to char on all sides until the eggplant is completely soft. Transfer to a colander and drain well. Allow to cool, then peel and roughly chop the eggplant and place in a food processor with $1^1/2$ tablespoons freshly squeezed lemon juice, $1^1/2$ tablespoons olive oil, 2 tablespoons tahini paste, 2 cloves crushed garlic, $1/2$ teaspoon ground cumin, and a good pinch each of salt and cracked black pepper. Process until smooth, transfer to a bowl and stir through $1/4$ cup (7 g) chopped fresh flat-leaf parsley. Can be made up to 3 days ahead and stored in an airtight container in the refrigerator. Makes about 1 cup (250 ml).

HUMMUS

Soak 125 g dried chickpeas overnight in plenty of water. Drain and transfer to a pan of boiling water. Cook, covered, over medium heat for 1 hour, or until tender. Drain and return to the pan. Add 1 tablespoon olive oil, 1 small finely chopped onion, 1 1/2 teaspoons ground cumin and a pinch of cayenne pepper to the pan and cook over high heat for 1 minute, or until aromatic. Place in a food processor and add 2 tablespoons freshly squeezed lemon juice, 1/2 cup (125 ml) olive oil and 3 crushed cloves garlic. Season with salt and process until smooth. Serve as is or add water if you prefer a thinner consistency. Can be made up to 5 days ahead and stored in an airtight container in the refrigerator. Makes about 2 cups (500 ml).

RED CAPSICUM AND WALNUT DIP

Quarter and seed 2 red capsicums. Place skin-side-up under a preheated grill and grill until the skin is blistered. Remove the skin. Heat 1 tablespoon olive oil in a pan, add 1 chopped onion and 1 crushed clove garlic and cook until soft. Stir in 1/2 teaspoon dried chilli flakes. Process 1/2 cup (60 g) walnuts until fine and add the capsicum, the onion mixture, 3 tablespoons olive oil, 2 teaspoons red wine vinegar and 1/4 teaspoon salt. Process until fine and almost smooth. Can be made up to 5 days ahead and stored in an airtight container in the refrigerator. Makes about 1 cup (250 ml).

TZATZIKI

Coarsely grate 1 unpeeled small green cucumber into a bowl. Add 1 cup (250 ml) thick Greek-style yoghurt, 2 crushed cloves garlic, 1 tablespoon red wine vinegar, 1 tablespoon olive oil, 1/4 teaspoon salt and 1/2 teaspoon cracked black pepper. Mix together well and serve. Can be made up to 3 days ahead and stored in an airtight container in the refrigerator. Makes about 1 1/2 cups (375 ml).

Opposite page
From top to bottom: Taramasalata; Feta spread; Baba ganouj.
This page
From top to bottom: Hummus; Red capsicum and walnut dip; Tzatziki.

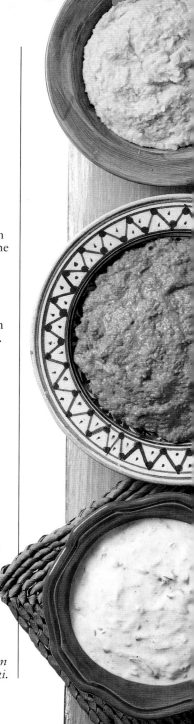

Pickled cauliflower

Preparation time:
10 minutes
Total cooking time:
10 minutes
Serves 4–6

2 cups (500 ml) white
  wine vinegar
1 tablespoon yellow
  mustard seeds
*1/2 teaspoon cumin
  seeds*
3 bay leaves
*3/4 cup (185 g) caster
  sugar*
400 g cauliflower, cut
  into florets

1. Put the vinegar, mustard seeds, cumin seeds, bay leaves and sugar into a pan. Stir over medium heat until the sugar has dissolved. Bring to the boil, then reduce the heat and add the cauliflower. Simmer for 4 minutes, or until just tender, but still firm.
2. Remove from the heat and leave the cauliflower to cool in the liquid. Serve chilled or at room temperature.

NUTRITION PER SERVE (6)
*Protein 1.5 g; Fat 0 g;
Carbohydrate 30 g; Dietary
Fibre 1 g; Cholesterol
0 mg; 600 kJ (145 cal)*

Note: To store, rinse a clean glass jar with a lid with boiling water and dry in a warm oven. Put the hot liquid and cauliflower in the jar, seal while hot and keep for up to 3 months unopened.

Saffron risotto-stuffed baby squid

Preparation time:
40 minutes +
  20 minutes cooling
Total cooking time:
20 minutes
Makes 16

*1/4 cup (60 ml) dry
  white wine*
2 cups (500 ml)
  vegetable stock
1/2 fennel bulb
1 leek, white part only
25 g butter
1 tablespoon vegetable
  oil
1 cup (220 g) arborio
  rice
pinch of ground saffron
16 baby squid hoods
  (approximately
  35 g each)
3 lemons, sliced

1. Combine the wine and stock in a pan and bring to a simmer over medium heat.
2. Cut the fennel and leek into thin slices and place in a heavy-based pan with the butter and oil. Cook, stirring, over medium heat for 4 minutes, or until softened. Add the rice and stir for 1 minute. Gradually add the hot stock mixture, a ladle at a time, stirring frequently until all the liquid has been absorbed before adding more. When the rice is tender add the saffron and season well with salt and cracked pepper. Spread the risotto onto a flat tray to cool slightly.
3. Stuff each squid with 2 teaspoons of risotto. Be careful not to overfill the squid or it may split during cooking. Secure the top of each squid with a toothpick. Preheat the oven to moderate 180°C (350°F/Gas 4).
4. Line a baking tray with foil, add the lemon slices and top with the stuffed squid. Cover and bake for 20 minutes, or until the squid are cooked and tender, turning once. Don't spoon the sauce over the squid as it is too bitter. Discard the lemon and juices after cooking, and serve the squid whole or cut into slices.

NUTRITION PER SERVE
*Protein 1.5 g; Fat 2.5 g;
Carbohydrate 12 g; Dietary
Fibre 1 g; Cholesterol
8.5 mg; 340 kJ (80 cal)*

*Pickled cauliflower (top)
with Saffron risotto-stuffed baby squid*

Stewed artichokes

Preparation time:
  15 minutes
Total cooking time:
  10 minutes
Serves 4

2 x 400 g cans globe
  artichokes, drained
10 strips preserved
  lemon, flesh removed
  and peel washed
*1/2 cup (125 ml) olive
  oil*
*1/2 cup (125 ml)
  vegetable oil*
*1/2 cup (125 ml) sherry
  vinegar*
1 tablespoon fresh
  lemon thyme leaves

1. Put the artichokes, peel, oils, vinegar and thyme in a pan with a lid. Cover and gently simmer for 10 minutes. Remove from the heat and cool the artichokes in the liquid.
2. Serve warm or cold by themselves, or as an accompaniment to grilled lamb pieces.

NUTRITION PER SERVE
*Protein 4 g; Fat 15 g;
Carbohydrate 3 g; Dietary
Fibre 6 g; Cholesterol
0 mg; 680 kJ (162 cal)*

Note: To successfully store the artichokes, sterilise the jar first by rinsing with boiling water and drying in a warm oven. Pour the artichokes and juice into the jar while still hot. Keep for up to 3 months unopened.
Note: Preserved lemons are fresh lemons preserved in salt, and are available from speciality food stores.

Mussel salad with saffron dressing

Preparation time:
  40 minutes
Total cooking time:
  30 minutes
Serves 4–6

250 g kipfler potatoes,
  unpeeled
20 black mussels
*1/3 cup (80 ml) dry
  white wine*
1 small onion, sliced
2 sprigs fresh thyme
2 bay leaves
*pinch of powdered
  saffron*
2 tablespoons sour
  cream
1 teaspoon chopped
  fresh parsley

1. Place the potatoes in a pan of cold, lightly salted water. Bring to the boil, then reduce the heat and simmer for 20 minutes, or until tender. Drain and cool.
2. Remove the beards from the mussels and scrub the shells. Discard any mussels that don't close when tapped. Place the wine, onion, thyme sprigs, bay leaves and half the mussels in a pot with a tight-fitting lid. Cover and cook over high heat, stirring once, for about 4 minutes, or until the mussels start to open. Take the mussels out of the pot with tongs as they open, making sure any unopened mussels are discarded. Cook the remaining mussels the same way, and leave to cool.
3. Strain the mussel cooking liquid, and reserve 1/4 cup (60 ml) of the liquid. While the liquid is still warm, stir in the saffron. Whisk in the sour cream and season well with salt and cracked pepper.
4. Slice the potatoes on the diagonal into 2 cm slices. Remove the mussels from their shell and discard the shells. Arrange the potato slices and mussels on a serving plate and pour on the saffron dressing. Sprinkle with chopped parsley and serve immediately.

NUTRITION PER SERVE (6)
*Protein 1.5 g; Fat 4.5 g;
Carbohydrate 6.5 g; Dietary
Fibre 1 g; Cholesterol
8.5 mg; 645 kJ (153 cal)*

*Stewed artichokes (top)
with Mussel salad with saffron dressing*

White fish salad with orange

Preparation time:
  30 minutes
Total cooking time:
  5 minutes
Serves 4

500 g firm white fish
  cutlets
2 tablespoons sherry
  vinegar
1 tablespoon orange
  juice
1 tablespoon olive oil
2 oranges
1/2 fennel bulb, thinly
  sliced
1/2 cup (80 g)
  marinated black
  olives

1. Remove the skin and bones from the cutlets. You will need about 250 g fish flesh, cut into large chunks (about 5 cm).
2. To make the vinegar dressing, mix together the vinegar, orange juice and olive oil, and season with salt and cracked black pepper.
3. In a pan, bring some lightly salted water to a simmer and gently place the fish into the water. Cook for 5 minutes, or until just cooked. Using a slotted spoon, carefully remove the fish from the water and, while still warm, cut into fine pieces. Add the fish pieces to the vinegar dressing and allow to cool.
4. Remove the skin and bitter white pith from the oranges. Using a small sharp knife, cut between the membranes to remove the orange segments.
5. In a bowl, toss together the slices of fennel, olives and orange segments, then spoon the fish mixture over the top of the salad. Season to taste with salt and cracked pepper. Serve at room temperature.

NUTRITION PER SERVE
*Protein 25 g; Fat 4.3 g;
Carbohydrate 6 g; Dietary
Fibre 2 g; Cholesterol
90 mg; 730 kJ (175 cal)*

Souvlakia

Preparation time:
  20 minutes +
  1 hour soaking +
  1 hour chilling
Total cooking time:
  10 minutes
Serves 4–6

1 kg boneless pork loin
  steak
1 tablespoon dried
  oregano
1/2 cup (125 ml) lemon
  juice
2 cloves garlic, crushed
1 tablespoon lemon
  juice, extra
1 tablespoon olive oil

1. Soak twelve 15 cm wooden skewers in water for 1 hour, or until they sink. This will ensure they don't burn during cooking.
2. Trim the pork steaks and cut them into 2 cm cubes. Put the oregano, lemon juice, garlic and 1/2 teaspoon cracked black pepper in a bowl. Add the pork, stir until well coated, then cover and refrigerate for 1 hour. Whisk the extra lemon juice, oil, 1/2 teaspoon salt and 1/2 teaspoon cracked black pepper in a small jug until well combined.
3. Thread the pork onto the prepared skewers.
4. Heat a lightly oiled barbecue hot plate until hot or heat a grill to its highest setting. Cook the souvlakia for 8–10 minutes, turning once during cooking. Place on a serving platter and pour the whisked lemon mixture over the top. Serve hot with tzatziki (page 49).

NUTRITION PER SERVE (6)
*Protein 40 g; Fat 6 g;
Carbohydrate 0.5 g; Dietary
Fibre 0 g; Cholesterol
80 mg; 885 kJ (210 cal)*

Note: The flavours will be enhanced if you marinate the pork a few hours ahead.

White fish salad with orange (top) with Souvlakia

Chop the bacon and mushrooms into small dice.

Cook the bacon and mushroom until tender and season well.

Borek of mushroom

Preparation time:
  40 minutes + cooling
Total cooking time:
  30 minutes per batch
Makes 24

4 rashers bacon
250 g mushrooms
1 tablespoon olive oil
1 onion, chopped
1/4 teaspoon paprika
6 sheets ready-rolled
  puff pastry, thawed

1. Chop the bacon and mushrooms into 1/2 cm cubes. Heat the olive oil in a non-stick frying pan over medium heat, and add the chopped onion and paprika. Fry the onion for 3 minutes without browning. Add the bacon and cook for a further 3 minutes. Add the mushroom and cook for 5 minutes more, or until all of the ingredients in the pan are tender. Season with plenty of salt and cracked black pepper, then spoon the mixture into a bowl. Set aside and allow to cool completely.

2. Using a 10 cm pastry cutter, cut four rounds out of each sheet of defrosted pastry. Place the rounds in the refrigerator to make handling them easier. Preheat the oven to moderately hot 200°C (400°F/Gas 6).

3. Spoon 1 tablespoon of the cold bacon and mushroom mixture into the centre of each round of pastry. Draw up the pastry to form four sides. To seal the borek, pinch the sides together firmly with wet fingertips. Repeat with the remaining pastry and filling.

4. Bake the borek on an oven tray covered with baking paper for 20–30 minutes, or until the pastry is golden and cooked. These borek are delicious eaten straight from the oven or served warm.

NUTRITION PER SERVE
Protein 5.5 g; Fat 10 g; Carbohydrate 15 g; Dietary Fibre 1 g; Cholesterol 18 mg; 760 kJ (180 cal)

Note: Although borek are traditionally thought to be of Turkish origin, they are also made in the Middle East and Eastern Europe. They are not always filled with mushroom; variations include meat, spinach and cheese, and the borek can be shaped into triangles, squares and circles. The pastry can also vary—shortcrust or filo pastry, or leavened dough can be substituted for the puff pastry if preferred.

Borek of mushroom

Spoon tablespoons of the mixture into the centre of each pastry round.

Draw up the pastry to form four sides and pinch the sides together to seal.

Cinnamon beef in cabbage leaves

Preparation time:
1 hour
Total cooking time:
20 minutes
Makes 8

1 tablespoon oil
2 onions, chopped
400 g beef mince
1/4 teaspoon ground nutmeg
1 teaspoon ground cinnamon
1/3 cup (50 g) pine nuts, lightly roasted
1 tablespoon chopped fresh parsley
1 tablespoon chopped fresh mint
8 large cabbage leaves

1. Heat the oil in a non-stick frying pan and fry the onions until soft. Add the beef mince, nutmeg, cinnamon and pine nuts. Season well with salt and cracked pepper. Cook for 5 minutes, or until the meat is cooked. Transfer to a bowl and cool. Stir in the parsley and mint.
2. Bring a large pan of lightly salted water to the boil. Put the cabbage leaves into the pan a few at a time and cook for 2 minutes, or until just tender, then run them under cold water. Cut out the thick stems with scissors.
3. Place spoonfuls of the mince mixture on each cabbage leaf and roll up, tucking in the sides of the leaves to form a parcel so that the filling is completely enclosed. Steam the rolls in a steamer over a pan of simmering water for 10 minutes, or until heated through. Serve warm or cold.

NUTRITION PER SERVE
Protein 12 g; Fat 12 g; Carbohydrate 2 g; Dietary Fibre 1.5 g; Cholesterol 30 mg; 685 kJ (165 cal)

White gazpacho

Preparation time:
45 minutes +
overnight chilling
Total cooking time:
2 minutes
Serves 4

1/2 cup (125 ml) chicken stock
1 slice bread, crust removed, diced
1 2/3 cups (300 g) large green grapes
1/2 cup (95 g) ground almonds
1 clove garlic, crushed
1/3 cup (80 ml) olive oil
1 1/2 tablespoons verjus or lemon juice (see Note)
green grapes, peeled, to garnish

1. In a small pan, heat the chicken stock and add the diced bread. Using a fork, mash the bread into the stock until all the liquid has been absorbed and the bread is soft. Cool.
2. In a food processor, purée the grapes and strain to remove skins and seeds. Place the ground almonds, garlic and bread in the cleaned food processor. With the motor running on low speed, gradually pour in the grape purée and olive oil. Season to taste. Strain through a fine strainer if you prefer a smoother texture. Add the verjus or lemon juice to freshen the soup.
3. Chill the soup completely and serve cold with sliced green grapes on the top. If the soup is too thick, add a little more chicken stock. For best results, leave the soup in the refrigerator overnight. Small servings are recommended as this dish is quite rich.

NUTRITION PER SERVE
Protein 6 g; Fat 35 g; Carbohydrate 15 g; Dietary Fibre 3 g; Cholesterol 0 mg; 1580 kJ (375 cal)

Note: Verjus is a sour liquid made mainly from unripe grapes.

Cinnamon beef in cabbage leaves (top) with White gazpacho

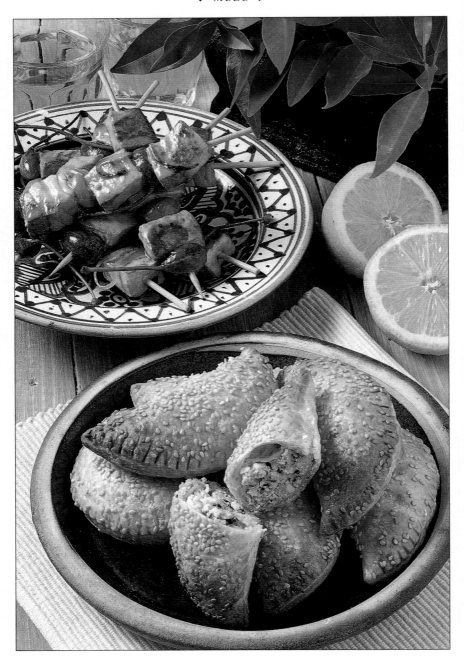

Tuna skewers with caperberries

Preparation time:
  20 minutes +
  1 hour soaking +
  30 minutes marinating
Total cooking time:
  10 minutes
Makes 8

250 g piece raw tuna
1/2 lemon
1 tablespoon lemon
  juice
1 tablespoon olive oil
16 caperberries
8 green olives, stuffed
  with an anchovy fillet

1. If you are using wooden skewers, soak them in cold water for 1 hour, or until they sink, to stop them burning while grilling. Cut the tuna into 24 even-sized cubes. Remove the rind from the lemon, avoiding the bitter white pith, and cut into thin strips. Combine the tuna, lemon rind, lemon juice and oil in a bowl.
2. Thread 3 pieces of tuna, 2 caperberries and 1 stuffed olive onto each skewer alternating each ingredient (that is, 1 piece of tuna, 1 caperberry, 1 tuna, 1 olive and so on).
3. Lay the tuna skewers in a non-metallic dish and pour on the lemon marinade. Refrigerate, covered, for 30 minutes.
4. Under a preheated grill, grill the tuna skewers for 1 minute on each side (there should be four sides to your tuna) for a total of 4 minutes, or until the tuna is cooked to your liking. Do not overcook or the tuna will dry out. Serve hot.

NUTRITION PER SKEWER
Protein 3 g; Fat 5 g; Carbohydrate 35 g; Dietary Fibre 0.5 g; Cholesterol 0 mg; 305 kJ (73 cal)

Cheese pastries

Preparation time:
  40 minutes
Total cooking time:
  20 minutes
Makes 16

160 g feta, grated
60 g ricotta
2 tablespoons chopped
  fresh mint
1 egg, lightly beaten
2 spring onions, finely
  chopped
2 tablespoons dry
  breadcrumbs
4 sheets ready-rolled
  puff pastry
1 egg, extra, lightly
  beaten
1 tablespoon sesame
  seeds

1. Preheat the oven to hot 220°C (425°F/ Gas 7). Lightly grease two baking trays.
2. Put the grated feta, ricotta, mint, beaten egg, spring onion, breadcrumbs and 1/2 teaspoon cracked black pepper in a bowl and mix with a fork to combine and break up the ricotta.
3. Using a 10 cm pastry cutter or saucer, cut rounds from the pastry sheets. Spoon level tablespoons of the cheese mixture into the centre of each round and lightly brush the edges with water. Fold over to enclose the filling, expelling any air, and firmly seal with the prongs of a fork to form a crescent shape. Brush with the extra egg and sprinkle with sesame seeds.
4. Put the crescents on the baking trays and bake for 15–20 minutes, or until the pastry is well browned and puffed. Should be served hot.

NUTRITION PER PASTRY
Protein 5.5 g; Fat 15 g; Carbohydrate 15 g; Dietary Fibre 0.5 g; Cholesterol 40 mg; 870 kJ (205 cal)

Note: The pastries can be prepared up to the end of step 3 two days ahead and kept, covered, in the refrigerator.

Tuna skewers with caperberries (top) with Cheese pastries

Green bean casserole

Preparation time:
25 minutes
Total cooking time:
35 minutes
Serves 6

500 g green beans
¹/4 cup (60 ml) olive oil
2 onions, chopped
1 clove garlic, chopped
3 tomatoes, diced
1 tablespoon tomato paste
¹/2 cup (125 ml) tomato purée
2 tablespoons chopped fresh flat-leaf parsley
¹/4 teaspoon sugar

1. Top and tail the beans, then cut in half.
2. Heat the oil in a large pan and cook the onion and garlic over low heat for 5 minutes, or until soft. Add the tomatoes, paste and purée, and cook over medium heat for 5 minutes.
3. Add the beans, parsley and sugar. Season well with salt and pepper. Stir until the beans are well coated, then cook, covered, over low heat for 25 minutes, or until the beans are tender, stirring three to four times. Delicious served hot or at room temperature.

NUTRITION PER SERVE
Protein 3.5 g; Fat 10 g; Carbohydrate 7 g; Dietary Fibre 4 g; Cholesterol 0 mg; 545 kJ (130 cal)

Rice-stuffed tomatoes

Preparation time:
40 minutes
Total cooking time:
50 minutes
Makes 8

8 medium tomatoes
¹/2 cup (110 g) short-grain rice
2 tablespoons olive oil
1 red onion, chopped
1 clove garlic, crushed
1 teaspoon dried oregano leaves
¹/4 cup (40 g) pine nuts
¹/4 cup (35 g) currants
¹/2 cup (30 g) chopped fresh basil
2 tablespoons chopped fresh parsley
1 tablespoon chopped fresh dill
olive oil, to brush

1. Lightly oil a large baking dish. Preheat the oven to warm 160°C (315°F/Gas 2–3). Slice the top off each tomato and reserve the tops. Spoon out the flesh into a bowl, place into a strainer to drain the juice and then finely dice the flesh. Reserve the juice and pulp in separate bowls. Drain the tomato shells upside-down on a rack.
2. Boil the rice in a pan of lightly salted water for 10–12 minutes, or until just tender. Drain and set aside to cool.
3. Heat the olive oil in a frying pan. Fry the onion, garlic and oregano for 8 minutes, or until the onion is tender. Add the pine nuts and currants and cook for a further 5 minutes, stirring frequently. Remove from the heat and stir in the basil, parsley and dill. Season to taste.
4. Add the onion mixture and reserved tomato pulp to the rice and mix well. Fill the tomato shells with the rice mixture, piling it up over the top. Spoon 1 tablespoon of the reserved tomato juice on top of each tomato and replace the tomato tops.
5. Lightly brush the tomatoes with the olive oil. Arrange them in a baking dish. Bake for about 20–30 minutes, or until cooked and heated through. Serve warm or cold.

NUTRITION PER SERVE
Protein 3 g; Fat 10 g; Carbohydrate 15 g; Dietary Fibre 2.5 g; Cholesterol 0 mg; 695 kJ (165 cal)

Green bean casserole (top) with Rice-stuffed tomatoes

Index